Beloved Disciples

EOLA JOHNSON

WARNER PRESS

Library of Congress Cataloging in Publication Data
Johnson, Eola

  Beloved Disciples

Includes bibliographical references.

1. Bible. N.T. John—Meditations. I. Title.

[BS2165.4.J64]   242   73-4539

ISBN 0 87162 154 1

Printed in the United States of America

I wish to dedicate this book
to my husband, Lloyd.

His love
concern
interest
understanding
cooperation
and encouragement
have meant much to me during this time of writing
and at all other times.

CONTENTS

Preface

All normal people believe that life is worthwhile. They want to live, and they want the good life. They hunger for it. They search everywhere. Even if the meaning of life escapes them, they feel that they should be able to find it.

We are born into a world that does not know God. We grow up in spiritual darkness, in bondage to sin. We are not happy. We are not satisfied. We yearn for something more. Somehow we know there must be a better way. In order to have this good life, special problems need to be solved. God can meet and answer these.

Fulfillment of needs and desires depends on the individual and his relationship with our heavenly Father. When you and I know him, love him, trust him, serve him, seek his guidance, and dedicate our lives to him, one by one, in his time, our needs are met; our questions and problems are answered.

Many times we have heard it said that Christ is the answer. This may seem rather vague, quite general. But it is true. A personal experience with God's divine Son in the life of each of us will bring us into a saving knowledge of our God and of his Christ. Jesus Christ has the words of the Father, and these are the words of life. When we accept the Son of God, not only as Savior, but as Lord of our lives, we have forgiveness of sin; guilt is banished. When we thus take him into our hearts and lives, we enter into the good life, the life that has no end, life with God.

To become one with Christ we must love him whom to love and know is life eternal. The Word of God—the Bible—is given that we may know him. As Christians grow in faith through meditation and study of the Word, as we mature as God wants and yearns for us to do, we will love truth and receive it. We will have an intuitive knowing.

God's Word is precious. Perhaps most loved by Christians is the Fourth Gospel, the Book of John. It is said to be the most philosophical, mature book in existence. John himself said that he wrote in order "that you may believe that Jesus is the Christ, the Son of God, and that believing you may have life in his name" (20:31). This Gospel is precious because the writer reveals the person of Jesus. Also this Gospel tells of the divinity of our Lord as our basis of faith and meets the spiritual needs of all people. For this reason it is known as the "spiritual Gospel."

Under the guidance of the Holy Spirit John was deeply perceptive and quick to realize spiritual truth. He drew love, light, and wisdom from the Master. He called himself "the disciple whom Jesus loved." He was not puffed up, thinking himself to be the only one loved by his Lord. John knew of Christ's deep love and concern for all *his* disciples. It was in humility that John knew himself as the beloved disciple. He responded to this love of Christ in a way that enabled him in his Gospel to give men "the heart of Christ," to be a herald reaching heaven for all.

Just as Jesus loved his immediate disciples—those who walked with him in his earthly ministry—he loves us. He prayed for us. John records this intimate prayer of Jesus to *his* Father in chapter 17. With the same humility that characterizes John, let us pray for guidance into truth that we may know and love Christ more.

As we read any portion of the Scriptures, certain passages stand out for us. This was true as I read John's Gospel.

When I was a child, my father loved to go for a spin in his first car. On long summer evenings and on weekends we would get in our trusty Maxwell and head for the open country. Dad was like a little pup. He was very curious and loved to investigate. When he saw a side road or a little country lane, he would turn off to see where it went, to see what was beyond the next rise. And I loved the prospect of seeing something new and different just as much as he did.

Later when I went with my husband in his work to small towns around the state, I would wander up one street and down another to see what interesting things I could discover.

In reading scriptures I often gain lessons for life from passages that ordinarily attract little notice. Sometimes these mean something very special to me. In these writings, based on the Gospel of John, I have wandered down a few byways. I have not avoided the better known verses, for I have included many. Those not included have been well covered by others more perceptive than I. Many of them literally speak for themselves.

It has been suggested that each day as we read we pick one verse or thought and meditate on it, making it ours for that day. In this little volume I have set forth special thoughts which came to me in connection with some favorite verses in John. This is not a study of John, but it could be used as thought starters for each day of one month. It is my hope and prayer that these thoughts will encourage you to study God's Word diligently and daily, so that you may receive and love the truth God has for you.

Remember, as you want the good life, infinitely more God wants you to have it, the real and only life. Remember, if you love and receive truth you, too, are Beloved Disciples!

Come with me and discover some of the things that John the beloved has said to us.

1. God Is Here

"To all who received him, who believed in his name, he gave power to become children of God" (John 1:12).

Read John 1.

JESUS said, "I am the way, and the truth, and the life; no one comes to the Father, but by me" (14:6).

Some tell us that everything that has given support in the past, including religion, is now shaking and that we cannot find God in this life. We are told that if we are to live sanely and with any degree of bodily health we must look for a complete new means of anchoring ourselves.

When Jesus said, ". . . I came that they may have life, and have it abundantly" (10:10), he referred to earthly life, continuing on through eternity. The abundant life is the good life, a life with God. He may be found here and now through his Son. We believe and receive him.

The song writer who wrote of God and him roaming the fields together knew the presence of God. Thousands through the years have found him, have walked with him. Thousands today believe and know his presence. Some, like Nicodemus the Pharisee, came to believe gradually; others, like the Samaritan woman at the well, believed at once. Still others, like the nobleman whose son was healed, believed solely because of the words of Jesus.

We, too, know the presence of God in various ways. He is very real to us in the communion of prayer. We petition him for ourselves and others. We lay our doubts and questions before him; we bring him our deepest needs. He answers because our faith is honest. He hears. He speaks to us. God is here.

As we have received him, believed on his name, and been empowered as children of God, we have entered the good life, the life abundant that Jesus came to give. Thank you, Father.

2. Fit For His Use

"Six stone jars were standing there, for the Jewish rites of purification, . . . Jesus said to them [the servants], 'Fill the jars with water.' And they filled them up to the brim" (John 2:6-7).

Read John 2:1-11; 2 Corinthians 4:1-7.

THIS filling of the jars with water took place at a wedding in Cana to which Jesus and the disciples were invited. Here he performed his first miracle by changing the water to wine.

In the Scriptures wine often represents joy. Ordinary things of life are represented by water. When you enter the life of God through Christ, God can change the mundane, routine, drab, to absolute joy and abundant life, if you will let him.

These jars were ready and waiting for use in purification rites. Christians, as "earthen vessels" are ready and waiting to be used for purification of the temple of God, which we are. (See 1 Corinthians 3:16.) We are cleansed by the washing of the word of God. Thus cleansed, as we grow in love, grace, and knowledge of our Lord, we are used for the purification of others by witnessing to them and encouraging them in the faith.

As we are filled to the brim with life's experiences transformed into joy, we have an abundant supply that overflows into the lives of others for distribution according to their needs.

This joy, this fruit of the Spirit, and other spiritual resources are not as the water in a motor-driven fountain which continually recirculates the same water. What God gives us is "a spring of water welling up to eternal life" (4:14) which is ever fresh and new. He is the inexhaustible Source of all our supply.

Our concern and helpfulness to others is not only a blessing to them, but it is for the glory of God. All we do and say is for him. In 2 Corinthians 4:6-7 Paul says that the treasure of light, life, and love was intrusted to us, the earthen vessels to which he likens us, to show that transcendent power belongs to God. We are vessels fit for his use. We are ever-thankful for his transforming power and the miracles he performs daily in our lives.

3. Share Your Encounter

"The woman left her water jar, and went away into the city" (John 4:28).

Read John 4:7-30; 39-43.

THE woman that Jesus met at the well in Samaria heard his words and believed. When she believed she wanted to go and tell. So she left the jar she had brought to fill with water and went into the city where the people were. She lost interest in physical things and went forth in search of spiritual things. She wanted others to know the Messiah also. She had had an encounter with God, and she wanted to share it. Because she testified of Christ, many believed in him.

Do you share your encounter with God with others so that they may believe? You have met him in his Word; he has come to you in worship, in the spoken word, in music, in the beauty of his handiwork, in life experiences. A beloved pastor said that worship is dynamic. It should result in action. Something must go with us out of the sanctuary as service to God. Another said that going to church is not serving. This is where we learn to serve. This is the beginning of service.

In order to serve him, in order to witness, we may have to leave what we are doing; we may have to go to another place. The heart of the woman of Samaria was filled with abundant joy. She was eager to pour out her story to all who would listen. So she went.

She had had a "mountaintop experience." She had left her water jar at the well, but she would return to it and other duties of her everyday life. We, too, have exhilarating experiences as we encounter God. But we cannot always stay on top of the mountain where the air is pure and our souls are free. We must return to the valley where responsibility, the needs of others, our lifework are. God expects this of us. But we can bring him with us. This is where our work is; this is where our service lies. This is where the people are; this is where we testify of him.

Let us share our encounter with God so that those with whom we come in contact will come to him and meet him in the Word. When they do, they, too, may say, "It is no longer because of your words that we believe, for we have heard for ourselves, and we know that this is indeed the Savior of the world" (v. 42).

4. The World Is Ready

"The fields are already white for harvest" (John 4:35).

Read John 4:31-38.

USUALLY when we speak of fields being white for harvest, we mean the crop is ripe or ready to be harvested. Actually this means it is past the harvest time. A field of grain is called "white" when the best time for harvesting is past, when the golden color of the grain begins to fade.

Jesus knew the hearts and minds of people, and he knew that for a long, long time they had needed what he came to give. He knew that God yearned for them, longed to gather them to himself. Jesus was telling the disciples to bring these needy souls into the Father's love.

I once attended a spiritual life retreat whose theme was "The World Is Ready, Are You?" The emphasis was that the greatest thing we can give a needy world is Christian unity. We were reminded that Jesus said, "I and the Father are one," and that this is the basis for our unity. We, too, through Christ are one with the Father. Through this union we are also one with other Christians. Such unity is brought about through love,

Christlike love, brotherly love. This bond of love will strengthen our cause, manifest itself to others as nothing else can. Of early Christians it was said, "See how they love one another!"

The world is ready to receive this love. Are you ready to give it? Do you have it to give? For a long, long time the world has been ready and waiting. The harvest truly is ripe for the reaping of love. The world tries everything; it looks everywhere. It wears itself out, but it does not know for what it searches. It does not know it must have love; it must have God.

Many of our young people search desperately, endlessly, tirelessly. We have witnessed the bizarre route this has taken them. We have seen the tragic results of their extremes. The harvest is overripe. Praise God, thousands are finding that which can end their search. They are becoming "Jesus' children." Let us pray that they will truly find him, the One who loves them, who has the words of life. Let us testify to them of his love.

5. Blessing Upon Blessing

"Jesus then took the loaves, and when he had given thanks, he distributed them to those who were seated; so also the fish, as much as they wanted" (John 6:11).

Read John 6:1-14.

HERE Jesus demonstrates in a miraculous way the spiritual truth of gratitude as the law of increase.

With a grateful heart for God's deliverance of the Israelites from the enemy, Samuel erected a stone and called it Ebenezer. His gratitude strengthened his trust, and he cried out, "Hitherto the Lord has helped us" (1 Sam. 7:12). It is as though this were an unfinished thought. Confidently he knew that if God had helped them in the past he would continue his watchful care. God's help in any situation is always definitely an improvement or an increase.

King David, too, was grateful. He deeply appreciated the love and companionship of his friend Jonathan, Saul's son. At one time in his reign, David said, "Is there any one left of the house of Saul, that I may show him kindness for Jonathan's sake?" (2 Sam. 9:1). Whenever thankfulness leads to kindness, increase or multiplication of good in the lives of the giver and the receiver is the result.

In instituting his memorial supper with his disciples, Jesus "took a cup, and when he had given thanks. . . ." (Matt. 26:27). When in our observance of the Lord's table we give thanks for all a loving God has provided, all that Christ in his atoning grace does for us, blessing will be added to blessing, ushering in the abundant life God planned for us.

On the occasion of the raising of Lazarus, at the door of the tomb, "Jesus lifted up his eyes and said, 'Father, I thank thee that thou hast heard me'" (John 11:41). Then he called Lazarus forth.

The idea of confident trust and expectation of good from the bountiful hand of God was impressed on me at an early age by our minister as he emphasized an important point in his message on prayer. I can see him yet. He knelt by a chair on the platform and said, "Always thank him for answering your prayer before you get up off your knees."

Much good may be added to our lives so that it may flow into the lives of others if we are truly thankful. Such blessing does not come through any merit of our own. It is as Paul says, "Thanks be to God, who gives us the victory through our Lord Jesus Christ" (1 Cor. 15:57). And for this victorious Christian life we are most grateful. Thank you, Father.

6. There Is A Garden

"Perceiving then that they were about to come and take him by force to make him king, Jesus withdrew again to the hills by himself" (John 6:15).

Read Matthew 26:36-47; John 18:1-9.

IN Warner Sallman's beautiful painting, "Keep Looking Up," Jesus is seated on a mound of earth looking at the sky or toward the distant hills. He was tremendously comforted and strengthened when he went alone for awhile to meditate and pray.

Because of his teaching and miracles, Jesus was popular with the people for awhile. In increasing numbers they followed him and wanted him to be their earthly king. This prevailing concept subjected him to much pressure, and he drew away to the hills by himself.

Later, when Jesus knew the time for leaving his disciples was drawing near, he went with them to the Garden of Gethsemane. His soul was sorrowful, and he prayed that his cup of suffering might pass. He also prayed that the Father's will be done. Because he and the Father were one, in times of deep personal need he felt the necessity of going alone with God, to hear his guiding, sustaining, loving words and sense his nearness.

Many Christian-oriented, church-related organizations plan regularly for retreats of one, two, or three days' duration once or twice a year. Members of these groups feel a need for spiritual renewal. They go to the mountains, the seashore, a quiet place apart from the usual scene of activity. Here they gain new insight, receive direction, plan for the future through meditation, prayer, study, conversation, solitude, rest.

On the program of a retreat that I attended this explanation was given: "Retreat means to draw, trace, and treat; draw from the 'well of water springing up into everlasting life,' retrace your identity where 'God created man in his own image,' and expect to treat yourself to renewal of your total being."

Just as groups of Christians need periodic spiritual infilling, so do individuals. They have personal problems which sorely tempt their souls. They have occupational difficulties which drain them nearly dry. God's children constantly encounter pressures from the world. They are expected to conform with enthusiasm to opinions of the day. They are offered places of authority in which they may see opportunities to influence significant endeavors for good. As individuals our times of renewal must be more frequent than those of the group. They may be needed several times daily. Besides the generally used and excellent means of Bible study, prayer and meditation, there are other ways of making life fuller, more pleasant, and easier.

In summer I get a happy start each day by touring my rose garden. As I breathe the fresh, cool air, I clip and discard stems from which the petals have fallen and gather a few choice blossoms for a beautiful new arrangement on the breakfast table. For those few moments the wonder and delight of nature create for me a world of beauty. As I enjoy the peace and quiet of early morning, I gain a sense of perspective and satisfaction. I am calmer and happier.

The world has a definite "gravity pull" for Christians. Lest we be sidetracked, let us go alone with God to seek his wisdom. As if on a mountaintop where the air is pure and invigorating, at these times we breathe the spiritual atmosphere of his presence. This helps keep us alive to him as we become involved again in the hurry and scurry of the day's work. As did Jesus, let us frequently "withdraw to the hills," and may we often go "where there is a garden" for the renewal we need.

7. Take Him Into Your Boat!

"They saw Jesus walking on the sea. . . . they were glad to take him into the boat, and immediately the boat was at the land to which they were going" (John 6:19, 21).

Read John 6:16-21; Romans 8:31-39; 1 John 4:1-6.

THE lives of many people are filled with the sad and frightening feeling that they are alone in the world. They are bowed low in sin and discouragement. They have listened to the wrong voices. Men have hurt and deceived them. They live in grief and pain. They are on a raging sea of resentment. Frequent storms threaten to swamp their boats, and they are often imperiled.

Time after time Jesus has come to them over the troubled waters, but they have not recognized him. When he is willingly taken into the boat—into the troubled heart—he is immediately responsible, for he is the Master of everything!

We cannot expect those of the world to hear him, for they are listening to confusing earthly voices. Christians are in tune with God, but they are not always aware of his presence. They, too, sometimes feel alone and are troubled and afraid. In their own efforts they try valiantly to run the race that is set before them, but they lose the way. They row around and around in circles. They need to take Christ into the boat, into the situation where the trouble is. When they gladly do this and surrender to his control, they will be well on the way to their destination.

In his transforming, compassionate grace Jesus enters our boat, our hearts, our lives. There is a great calm, and we are victorious. Through Christ in us we are overcomers, for he that is in us is greater than he that is in the world. God is for us, and none can stand against us. You and God are an overwhelming majority.

There were periods of doubt and questioning among the disciples, and some "drew back and no longer went about with him." Jesus asked the twelve, "Will you also go away?" Peter answered, "Lord, to whom shall we go?" (6:66-68). Why should he turn away? Jesus has the words of eternal life; he is the Holy one from God, the Christ. Why should anyone seek elsewhere for help, care, fulfillment of his needs?

It was my privilege last year to hear a beautiful, vibrant Christian young woman speak in a women's meeting on the general subject of joy.

"If she can be joyful, I can, too," was the remark made afterward by an elderly woman who had just lost her husband.

The speaker had two small children, both with a medically incurable disease. Yet she is used of God to encourage and strengthen the faith of other Christians.

When questioned regarding this, she radiantly replied, "I've placed them in God's hands. What better place is there? Where else is there better care?"

Oh, Christians, trust him, expect him to bring you through your trials to your destination. He can and will if you take him joyously into your boat!

8. New Every Morning

"The bread of God is that which comes down from heaven, and gives life to the world" (John 6:33).

Read John 6:25-51.

WE read in Exodus 16 that morning by morning the Israelites gathered the manna, "The bread which the Lord has given you to eat," each as much as he could eat. The bread was faithfully and regularly supplied by their loving God each day for forty years, or until they came to a habitable land.

Of God's generosity and bountiful provisions, the prophet Jeremiah says:

> *The steadfast love of the Lord never ceases,*
> *his mercies never come to an end;*
> *they are new every morning;*
> *great is thy faithfulness.*
> —Lamentations 3:22-23

In the beginning was God. In the beginning was love. We love him because he first loved us and with strong cords of love drew us to himself.

Of God, the writer of Proverbs said:

> *I love those who love me*
> *and those who seek me diligently find me.*
> —Proverbs 8:17

Meeting God early in love and trust and grateful recognition of his blessings, brings hope to us, even hope of everlasting glory.

Job in his troubles, cried out:

> *God has cast me into the mire,*
> *and I have become like dust and ashes.*
> —30:19
> *I have sewed sackcloth upon my skin,*
> *and have laid my strength in the dust.*
> —16:15

Although Jeremiah lamented after the fall of Jerusalem, he also had hope.

When Scarlett O'Hara, in *Gone with the Wind,* returned to Tara after Yankee troops had gone through the land, she found it deserted and in ruins. Hungry, lonely, and in despair she wandered through the grounds. The garden was mostly trampled and uprooted. She wept and threw herself on the ground, clutching the dirt. Her hand touched a radish. She raised up and ate it ravenously. Then she brushed away her tears, stood up, threw back her shoulders, and started toward the house.

"I'll cry tomorrow!" she exclaimed as, with courage and hope she began her task of restoring Tara and remaking her life.

We, too, may be sorrowful, but if we can put off crying until tomorrow and meet each new day optimistically, looking for God's goodness, we may have no need or time for crying. His blessings like dew, as the manna, are falling. Let us find this bread of God coming down from heaven to give us life! Let us claim each new day as one that God has made and rejoice and be glad in it!

9. Light Shines
On The Gate

"If any man's will is to do his will, he shall know whether the teaching is from God" (John 7:17).

Read John 7:14-17; 16:12-15; Ephesians 2:1-10.

JESUS Christ's purpose in his total ministry was to do the will of God. More than anything else the Father wanted Jesus to bring light and everlasting life to men everywhere. Accordingly, he gave Jesus the authority to do this by giving him divine wisdom and words of life.

When Jesus left his disciples, he asked the Father to send them the Comforter, or the Holy Spirit. The Spirit ministers to the world, and he ministers to Christians. He convicts the world of sin, righteousness, and judgment.

An important ministry of the Spirit to Christians is to guide them into truth. Under his guidance when we read the Word of God, we truly hear what God is saying, and it has deep meaning to us. We recognize that these are words to live by, words of everlasting life.

We are God's children. Knowing and loving us, he created in us a yearning toward himself. Some have called this the spark of God within us. Since Adam and Eve were cast out of Eden, they have been longing to return. With Adam and Eve representing all of mankind, this is true. We have seen the thousands of ways this yearning is manifested by a world that is lost and desperately searching. Mostly, it does not know that it is looking for God and his way of life. A long time ago Jesus said that he who hungers and thirsts for righteousness shall be filled. Oh, what blessing, what happiness, to be satisfied with God's righteousness, his truth for our lives! All to whom the Spirit ministers through his guidance find the life God has planned for them.

Do you know that God has a plan for you? He has a plan for everyone, and this is that each may have the abundant life that Jesus came to give. Keep looking to the truth revealed by the Spirit. Where its light is shining we may enter the gate, narrow though it be, beyond which lies the way that leads to this joyous life with God. This is a wide place of freedom. We are no longer under bondage of any kind. We can lay aside the sin and weights that formerly burdened us.

Just as Jesus set himself to do the will of his Father, Christians desire to do God's will and work. Because God knew us, he knew that we would respond in this way to his gift of the good and plenteous life. So he prepared good works for us to do before we knew him. We are his workmanship, and he created us to function for him. If we are in his will, as Jesus said, we will know whether his teaching, or any teaching, is from God. We will know that what we need to know about God can be known, for it is revealed in his Word.

34

10. Stars In A Dark World

"Nicodemus, who had gone to him before, and who was one of them, said to them, 'Does our law judge a man without first giving him a hearing and learning what he does?' " (John 7:50-51).

Read John 7:37-52; Philippians 2:12-18; Hebrews 4:14-16.

NICODEMUS did not fully believe in Jesus' deity all at once. His faith was progressive. John speaks of him three times and each time Nicodemus has grown in his faith in Jesus.

Our faith, too, may be in the process of becoming. It may be only as a mustard seed in the beginning.

"Don't be discouraged if you're not a St. Francis of Assisi overnight!" one pastor said in a message on patience.

In the parable of the growing grain, Jesus said that the kingdom of heaven grows as the grain: first the blade, then the ear, then the full grain in the ear (Mark 4:26-29).

Nicodemus came to Jesus first by night, for he was afraid. He was a Pharisee, a member of the Sanhedrin, the ruling council. As yet he had no real faith, but he had many questions which were unanswered. Unlike the others, he was not against Jesus, but he could not say for sure he was the Messiah.

Later at the Feast of the Tabernacles, when the people were divided because of Jesus, Nicodemus defended him in the council. His was the only voice in Jesus' favor. He was courageous and open.

Through the years there have been many believers, and today there are those who stand firmly for Christ, but they are a minority. They live amid great darkness of unbelief. Many around them claim to know God and profess Jesus, but their lives are filled with seemingly unsolvable problems. They band themselves together in spiritual growth groups trying to help each other find solutions, but they refuse to submit to the authority of God's will, and so their problems continue. Jesus traced all doubts of his divinity to similar unwillingness.

When activated by the Holy Spirit, chosen ones of God produce an effective witness that echoes down the ages, even through eternity. As with Nicodemus, their testimony shines as stars in a darkened world.

What do you do to witness for Christ? Come often before his throne seeking guidance within his will. Yield your lives completely to him. As he has promised, you will receive mercy and find grace to help in time of need. You may be an instrument of the Divine to help some hungering one to confess his Lord and to grow to be like him.

At the death of Jesus, when the others were gone, Nicodemus came with Joseph of Arimathea and some of the women to claim the body and prepare it for burial. He brought much costly spice and linen (19:39). His love for Jesus had gradually grown so that without hesitation, and caring not what others would say or do, he identified completely with the Master and his cause.

If we would have our love for Christ strengthened, come to him, not secretly in the dark, but openly and witness boldly for him. In his own way, he will reveal himself to us, and our faith will progress, growing into a "full grain in the ear."

11. He's Been There!

"When he has brought out all his own, he goes before them, and the sheep follow him, for they know his voice" (John 10:4).

Read Psalm 23.

ON some school days during the winter our school superintendent leads the way for the children to go to school. When the roads are icy or filled with snow, he gets up very early in the cold darkness and drives over all the routes the school buses normally take. Then he knows just what the conditions are and whether the drivers will be able to bring the children to school safely. He then determines whether school will be in session. He is able to do this, for he knows the way. He has gone before.

Are you going someplace? God has already been there. He knows the way, and he will guide you.

The Scriptures mention many of the unnumbered places where God has been and where he will lead you. He will go before you into green pastures, still waters, on paths of righteousness, through the valley of the shadow of death. He will take you to his house along paths of love and faithfulness. He will take you through trouble into his shelter. Together you will go through deep water and walk through fire. He will lead you to mountain heights and to springs of living water.

God has gone before to prepare the way, and he takes you through joy and pain. He will allay your fears and grant you his peace. As the Navajo Indian by his evening campfire, you, too, can sing the ancient peace chant: "Thy light shines on my pathway and I have peace. . . . Thy light shines before me and I have peace. Thy light shines behind me and I have peace."

We are thankful that he goes before us and comforted to know always that he is with us. What blessing there is in knowing that he follows after, catching us when we slip, picking us up when we fall, guarding us from harm!

God is everywhere and present always. We are completely surrounded by his presence. How much better to go the way he has planned than the precarious one we may choose for ourselves. So let us trust him and yield our lives to his control. He has been where we are going.

12. Nothing But The Facts

"Lazarus is dead" (John 11:14).

Read John 11:5-16; 1 Corinthians 13:12;
Philippians 3:12.

WHEN interviewing witnesses, Sergeant Friday, detective of TV fame, wants only the facts. Sometimes these are hard to discern. People relate what they see and hear to what they already know and have experienced. Resulting information is varied, but all is given as fact.

A child in looking up at a thermometer may see the registered temperature a few degrees different than a taller person looking squarely at the instrument. The eye-level reading is more accurate.

When I ride with my husband and feel that he is driving too fast, I look over at the speedometer from the right-hand front seat. Invariably it indicates from five to ten miles per hour more to me than to him when he looks straight ahead at it.

Besides this type of distortion of facts, the many circumstances of life present numerous others. Much of what the world calls realism is misrepresentation of truth. Life is so filled with distortion that many completely lose sight of truth. Many more never know reality. This is tragic, for God wants us to have the good and true life, to live in the truth that sets us free from anything that limits our spiritual growth.

Some instances of changing the truth are given in the Bible. During his last appearance to his disciples before his ascension, Jesus questioned Peter. In John 21:23 we read, "The saying spread abroad among the brethren that this disciple was not to die; yet Jesus did not say to him that he was not to die, but, 'If it is my will that he remain until I come, what is that to you?' "

Some of the purpose of this passage is to teach us to listen, to get the facts, and to retell accurately. To listen is to try to hear, and this requires a willingness, an effort, an action on our part. Hearing is the successful result of true listening.

Jesus taught his followers to face facts. "Lazarus is dead," he said. He wasn't sleeping, as they supposed. Then he said, "I am glad that I was not there, so that you may believe."

Certainly as they witnessed the raising of Lazarus their faith in the Master was strengthened. When we face facts, see people and things as they are, we are better able to see Christ's authority in the transformation that often takes place. Our attitudes and methods are more accurate and fair in dealing with them.

God wants us to tell his truth accurately. We have this truth from his Son, from the apostles, and other biblical writers. It is our responsibility as Christians to go and tell it.

I was impressed with the picture on the cover of a paperback book, *Tell It Like It Is*. One earnest little man with an open Bible in one hand is sitting on another little man lying on his back. The aggressive one has his mouth open and his hand on his victim's chest or throat. The prone man, red of face, his tongue out, looks a bit worried.

We are not to be this violent, but we need to know what we are talking about. A positive, confident manner really pays off, and nothing catches on like enthusiasm! Our pastor makes a tremendous impact on youth. Through the years he has brought them in from the highways and byways, from lives of sin and despair. He takes a very definite and earnest stand, and his zeal never lags as he teaches them. Because he really believes what he teaches and knows his subject well, many have become flaming evangels under his ministry.

Many decisions are required as we serve God. When making decisions it is wise to wait until we have all the facts. How can we know when all are in and which data is fact? Depending only on ourselves, we see dimly. We know only in part, for we have not yet obtained wisdom, maturity, righteousness. In his wisdom God gave us the Holy Spirit. Let us continually seek his guidance.

Because Christ has made us his own, we will press on to make God's righteousness ours. We will see face to face, form proper attitudes, make decisions, and witness in truth for him. If with all our hearts we want to put away childish things and put on maturity, we will grow up in Christ!

13. Continuous Entry

"I believe that you are the Christ, the Son of God, he who is coming into the world" (John 11:27).

Read John 11:17-27; 15:1-8.

THE coming of Christ into the world is a continuous process. In Colossians 1:27 we read, "Christ in you, the hope of glory." Because Christ is in us we have life and love that never end. Because we are branches of the true vine we bear much fruit in the lives of others through his life in us.

God the Father never leaves himself without witnesses to the truth that Christ lives throughout eternity. There were those who brought the law, the prophets, the kings. Then John came, preparing the way for Christ who was the truth itself. Then came the apostles and other leaders of the early church. Christians have witnessed through the years and are witnessing today. Because of their faithful testimony Christ continues to come into the hearts and lives of thousands today, and they will let his light shine from their lives into those yet to come. Thus, the life of Christ goes on. He continues to come into the world till the end of the age when his followers will be caught up with him in the air, and they shall be with him forever.

Christ continues to come in the lives of individuals. As we grow in Christ and mature in our spiritual lives, learning and living more and more of truth that God has for his own, the Christ continues to come. As our Christian lives develop and unfold, Christ manifests himself through us ever more fully. He has ever been coming, he continues to come, and he evermore will come—for he is eternal!

14. Cleanse Me!

"Why was this ointment not sold for three hundred denarii and given to the poor?" (John 12:5).

*Read John 12:1-11; Mark 9:14-29;
Psalm 119:9-11.*

GREAT contrast is pictured in this scene in the home of Jesus' friends.

Before the Feast of the Passover in Jerusalem Jesus stopped for a few days of rest and comfort in Bethany. In the midst of beauty and warm expression of love, the smoldering resentment and bitterness of Judas asserted itself like a chilling blast or an icy wave. That he would dare or be able to speak in criticism in such an atmosphere of devotion causes the meanness of his heart to stand out more clearly. He could not stand to see the loss of so much money, for he was a covetous man. He did not care if his words crushed Mary's spirit of love and indicated that he thought the Master undeserving of such a costly gift. Many scholars believe that this is when Judas decided to betray Jesus to the chief priests. Why not? He could never become wealthy or amount to much under such a lowly leader!

Do we betray Christ? This is often done in innocence, unconsciously, through weakness. It was in a moment of weakness that even Peter, one of the Twelve, denied him. So it can happen, even to Christians. Purposely denying or betraying him is a far greater sin. Judas' act was premeditated. He reaped the reward of his wickedness. Not even seeking forgiveness, he did away with himself, thus destroying his soul. His life is a constant warning to Christians so that they may not sin against God.

In his greed Judas seemed to be concerned for the poor. In our lives seeming good thoughts or appearances can sometimes be a cover-up for something else.

A story is told of a butcher who would put his thumb on the edge of the scales when he weighed meat. His friendly, jolly manner falsely indicated that he was friendly and interested in serving his customers well. His dishonest practice went unnoticed until the keen eyes of a child detected it. She asked why he did this.

"He's taking from his soul and adding to his wallet," her mother replied.

"How can a young man keep his way pure?" the psalmist asks. Then he answers his own question, "By guarding it according to thy word."

If our ways are not pure there are reasons why this is so. Perhaps it is because of ignorance of truth or unbelief.

In partial darkness, the father of the boy with a dumb spirit cried out, "I believe; help my unbelief!"

Because we are still growing as Christians and Christ's manifestation in and through us is progressive, there is always a measure of unbelief or darkness in us. We can not overcome this alone. We need God's help to blot out the darkness of our ways. The light of his truth can flood these areas of our minds and hearts searching out the sin that is hidden there.

If we truly desire to be clean before God, our prayer can be that of the song writer:*

Search me, O God, and know my heart today.
Try me, O Savior, know my thoughts, I pray;
See if there be some wicked way in me;
Cleanse me from every sin, and set me free.

We can be free from ignorance, resentment, bitterness, and come into the light of his truth where there's warmth, beauty, and love. May his word be found in our hearts so that we won't sin against him.

---

*"Cleanse Me," by Edwin Orr and John McNeil.

15. Made Whole
To Make Whole

"Many even of the authorities believed in him, but for fear of the Pharisees they did not confess it, lest they should be put out of the synagogue" (John 12:-42).

Read John 12:35-43; Hebrews 11-12:2.

HEBREWS 11 reads like the Hall of Fame or a spiritual Who's Who. The men and women we read about there were people of God, filled with faith and courage. God used them, and their influence continues to inspire and encourage believers. God needs bold workers and witnesses to act and speak confidently for him today. We are representatives of Christ. God makes his appeal through us. We are reconciled that we may become reconcilers. God is depending on us to bring wandering, fearful ones into his everlasting kingdom. Ours is a grave responsibility, requiring definite, bold testimony.

Instructing Timothy and the church, Paul said, "God did not give us a spirit of timidity, but a spirit of power" (2 Tim. 1:7).

At the ascension Jesus told his disciples that they would receive power when the Holy Spirit came to them.

I once viewed a film, "Back to Jerusalem" which told of the coming of the Spirit to breathe life into the church. I will never forget the faces of the disciples as they left that place following this wonderful Pentecost experience. They were aglow with the light of expectation, power, and great commitment. They radiated the love and glorious will of God. These men were ready and able to cause others to believe.

As in the days of the early church, the Holy Spirit is still our guide and always will be the divine guide into all truth. We can know the truth of the Scripture; we can know much of what is to come. God has said that this is so. As we live according to the truth thus revealed, it becomes a part of our lives. Our faith is strong and we, too, can be aglow with the light of the Spirit. We can come to God with confidence and receive mercy and grace to help in time of need. Where we are yet weak, we can be made strong. We can help others in their needs and show them the way to God.

16. Pick Up Your Towel

"Jesus . . . laid aside his garments, and girded himself with a towel" (John 13:3-4).

Read John 13:1-17; Luke 22:24-27.

KNOWING who he was, Jesus picked up a towel and washed the disciples' feet.

When the time was drawing near for his betrayal, Jesus had met with his disciples secretly for their last supper. There may not have been a servant to remove their sandals and wash the dust of the street from their feet.

Perhaps they felt a little strange, for it was a breach of Eastern custom to sit at the table with unwashed feet. But none offered to wash another's feet. They were concerned instead with something else. They were arguing over who among them was the greatest. But Jesus rose from the supper to perform this menial task.

When he had finished, he came back to the table and said that he had given them this example so that they would do as he had done. He used symbolism to teach two important aspects of humility. When he told them they ought to wash one another's feet, any humble act or service was symbolized.

In preparing for the foot washing, Jesus removed his outer garment, leaving only the under tunic. This was the attire of a servant. Thus, he symbolized that his followers were to become as servants as they ministered to one another. They were to regard themselves as lower in esteem than those they served.

Jesus was willing to do this in order to meet the needs of others. He knew that his Father had given him all things, all authority. He had left heaven's glory which he had shared with his Father. He was going to God, yet he humbled himself. He became a servant.

As children of the King, joint heirs with Christ, members of the royal family of God, are we willing to become slaves to meet the needs of others? Would we put on the garb of a slave, make ourselves lower than those we would serve?

"She even carried out my garbage!" said a friend about the way a friend had helped in caring for her and her home during her illness. By humbling herself, donning the role of a servant, this friend was a source of comfort and help in a time of need. Her love came to bless and heal.

The dynamics of God's kingdom are the very opposite of those of worldly kingdoms. In the heavenly realm we rise in proportion to our descent.

In testifying to Jesus, John the Baptist said, "He must increase, but I must decrease" (John 3:30).

As he went about baptizing with the water of repentance John said he wasn't worthy to carry Christ's sandals (Matt. 3:11). In humility he served. In humility he prepared for the coming of the Lord!

Someone has said, "All truly great men are humble." In humility the self is denied—even put to death. Christ increases, for he lives ever more fully in the new creature that emerges. God is glorified. Others are served.

17. Even As He Loved

"Love one another; even as I have loved you. . . . By this all men will know that you are my disciples, if you have love for one another" (John 13:34-35).

Read John 13:31-35; 15:9-17; Romans 8:35-39; 1 Corinthians 13.

TO love as Christ loves us is to have a selfless love. To love our neighbor as ourselves may call for this kind of love, but some of us do not love ourselves very much. Christ loved us enough to die for us. This is the type of love to which he calls us. He said, "Greater love has no man than this, that a man lay down his life for his friends."

God so loved the world that he gave his Son. He gave us this most precious gift, the one dearest to his heart, that we might be brought back into a right relationship with him, a love and saving relationship. Oh what love! Jesus, the glorious Son, was willing to leave his heavenly home with his Father to suffer and die for us! He used this love as a pattern for his followers.

It is not often that Christians lay down their bodily lives for their friends, but self can die daily in acts of love for others. Self is a die-hard. He is king of life. He is not dethroned easily—only by God's grace, prayer, setting our minds, and willing it so. From dedicating our lives to serving others for the glory of God, a love for God and others will grow. Self, with his desires and demands, will diminish as Christ, the new king, lives and loves through us.

Such love knows no boundaries. Love has been described as a feeling of goodwill toward others. Surely Christians can want what is best for all people. Surely they want all people to be happy, to live as God wants them to live. Their thoughts, prayers, and actions can be for this.

A friend once said, "Love is a free-flowing, inexhaustible fountain going out to all in comforting warmth and interested concern."

"Interested concern" — this leads to compassion, which is concern that leads to action. Our Lord is compassionate; he is where compassion is.

Love is called "a many-splendored thing." It also has many strengths. In love, self-built walls of fear and sensitivity can be broken down and bridges can be built across any gulf that separates us from our brothers. Our love can be a rushing tide, needing no bridges, for the blessing it bears can go to our brother on the crest of its waves. It has been said that love causes ordinary men to do *extra*-ordinary things. Love's greatest strength is its endurance, for it never fails.

Followers of Jesus keep his commands. We are commanded to love. Keeping his sayings is a test of discipleship. This is also the best witness. Of early Christians it was said, "How they love one another!"

Let us love one another, even as Christ loves us. Let us think of others first, give of ourselves to them.

18. A Place To Stand

"He lifted up his eyes to heaven and said, 'Father . . .' " (John 17:1).

Read John 17:1-5; Philippians 3:1-16; Matthew 6:25-33.

JESUS said, "Go into all the world and preach the gospel to the whole creation" (Mark 16:15).

Commenting on this passage in *Guideposts,* Paul Tournier, Swiss Christian psychiatrist, said that in order to go, we must have a place from which to go, meaning that we must be right with God ourselves before we can go and tell others about him.

The world was lost in sin. Men had strayed far from God. They drifted—aimless, frightened, and insecure. Jesus came that they might have a place to stand. He said that through him they could come to the Father and see and know him.

Christians have availed themselves of this saving knowledge of God whom to know is to love and serve. Their aim is to glorify him in every thought and act. But often they are weak; they haven't fully attained this lofty estate. They, like others, long for a place where they can rest and be safe, a "home" from which to go into the world.

Speaking of the vast urbanization of our country, Foy Valentine said, "We were rooted in the soil, but now from the cradle to the grave we roll around on the pavement."

City-bound folk watch westerns on TV, thus expressing and partly satisfying a longing to go home, to return to the soil, to the way things used to be. We all have places we like to go where we are comforted, where we feel at home. It may be to the old hometown, to the home of a friend, or to grandmother's house. If you are a grandmother, you may still want to go home.

But we can not go home again, not really. Nor would we want to, for in vainly expending energies in attempting to return fully, we forfeit the future. Then where can we go?

Paul said, "Forgetting what lies behind . . . I press on toward the goal of the prize of the upward call of God in Christ Jesus" (Phil. 3:13-14).

We are in a world of continual change, pushing always forward, never backward. We must go on, but we can cushion the shock of too much rapid change in the comfort of temporarily returning to the past occasionally. But our main thrust must ever be the upward call of Christ.

As Christians, we are rooted and grounded in Christ. But we need to pray for others and for ourselves as Jesus did. We must bring to God our fears and doubts, our unbelief, and the measure of darkness that is in us. In thus communing with him we learn the way he wants us to go.

19. From Fear To Faith

"The maid who kept the door said to Peter, 'Are you not also one of this man's disciples?' He said, 'I am not' " (John 18:17).

Read John 18:12-27; 19:12-16; Acts 12:12-17.

ARE we like the little girl in a story who, when she went out, took her umbrella even though it was a bright sunny day. Many in her community had prayed for rain to end the long drought, and she expected rain.

Or do we doubt or become amazed when God answers our prayers? Those gathered in the home of John Mark's mother disbelieved when the maid told them that Peter was at the gate, although they had been praying for his release from prison. To be unbelieving in such instances is to have a form of godliness but to deny its power, to deny the Christ who intercedes for us (2 Tim. 3:5).

If we have no depth of belief, no real conviction, we may be swayed by whatever is popular. Our thoughts and actions are as the crowd before Pilate crying out, "Crucify him! . . . We have no king but Caesar."

Fear and faith are said to be the opposite poles of the same thing, the negative and positive degrees of belief. Jesus said that our faith should be as that of a little child. A child is trusting. His faith is wholehearted. He has not had a lifetime in which to build up fears and dreads. In simple faith he trusts, he believes. Because we older ones lack this faith, we have a measure of unbelief. We sometimes deny our Lord.

It was in fear that Peter denied Christ. He feared the servants and he feared the authorities. He was so afraid that he invoked an oath on himself with its attendant dangers and testified to a falsehood.

The awful responsibility for rejecting Christ is in proportion to the light received. God spoke to men through his Son giving them light and life eternal. To be given light and then to refuse it by ignoring his words, by refusing to read them, or by disbelieving them is to be judged by them. In this judgment we are threatened with the wrath of God, condemnation, and death (John 3:18, 36; 8:24).

But our loving, gracious heavenly Father eagerly waits and is quick to restore us when through weakness we wander afar. The glory of his grace is well illustrated in Peter's later life. When he repented, he was restored and became a flaming evangel for the one he had denied. God's grace is sufficient for you and me. He will forgive our fears and unbelief. Then, as we grow in grace and when our faith is strong, we can be as George Mueller whose eyes were not on the fog but on the living God when he prayed for the fog to lift on an important sea voyage. The fog was removed.

Let us not be fearful or in unbelief deny our Christ. But let us keep our eyes on the living God and believe!

20. Somewhere Listening

" 'For this I was born, and for this I have come into the world, to bear witness to the truth. Every one who is of the truth hears my voice.' Pilate said to him, 'What is truth?' " (John 18:37-38).

Read John 18:33-40; 16:12-15; 14:15-17, 25-26.

PILATE may have been a cynic, having no regard for truth or any personal concern over it. But his question is one that true believers ask sincerely—What is truth?

Even those with no professed belief in Christ are seeking. God has placed within them a yearning toward himself. They do not know that in their restlessness, their hunger, they are seeking God. They try everything, believe anything except Jesus Christ, whom to know is to know God. In a sense they are asking, "What is truth?" But with the crowd they cry, "Not this man, but Barabbas!"

Jesus said that truth is God's word (John 17:17). He had the words of God and gave them to the disciples as they were ready to receive and understand them. He left them with the promise of the Holy Spirit who would reveal more truth. The Spirit would not speak on his own authority, but would declare the words of

God as he heard them from Christ. And he would help them remember what Christ had said to them. He would always be with them, for he would be in them.

So we see that Jesus did not leave his followers comfortless or without help in gaining knowledge of more truth. We, too, are his followers and have the abiding Presence within. As we hunger and thirst after his righteousness we will be filled. The Holy Spirit is the Spirit of truth who still guides us into truth. The Spirit guided the writers of the New Testament to speak Christ's words to us.

We read that faith comes by hearing, and hearing by the Word of God (Rom. 10:17). So then let us ever listen for God's word spoken from the Scriptures through the Spirit. As we read, let us hear what he is saying, for his word is the answer to the age-old question, What is truth?

21. Care For Your Own

"When Jesus saw his mother, and the disciple whom he loved standing near, he said to his mother, 'Woman, behold, your son!' Then he said to the disciple, 'Behold, your mother!' And from that hour the disciple took her to his own home" (John 19:26-27).

*Read John 19:25-27; 1:40-42, 45, 46;
1 Timothy 5:3-16.*

JESUS cared for his own. Even as he hung on the cross he arranged for John to care for his mother.

According to New Testament teaching, all Christians are to care for their own. It is the duty first of the family to care for their members who are in need. Only if this cannot be done does it become the duty of the church. A lengthy section of 1 Timothy 5 is devoted to the enrolling of widows. The churches were to provide only for those in need and those having no other means.

"Behold, your son!" "Behold, your mother!" These words remind us of the brotherhood among Christians. Jesus regarded John as his brother. Therefore, John was also Mary's son, and Mary was John's mother.

John, in caring for her, was caring for his own, thus fulfilling an obligation of a Christian family man.

I recall a conversation with dear friends who live some distance from us and whom we do not see often. In our joy of being together again we spoke of the great bond of love between Christian friends often being stronger than that between blood brothers. And we were happy that this is so.

When I told my stepdaughter about my brother living in poor circumstances alone in a distant large city, she said, "What will become of him? Is he to be lost there to become one of the faceless men of the masses?"

She scarcely knew him, yet she was concerned; she cared for her Christian brother. I was impressed by her attitude. Steps were taken whereby my brother has a better life and no longer is alone. And he never forgets that others care for him.

In 1 Timothy 5 Paul says that members of families have spiritual duties to one another. When Andrew, a disciple, found his messiah, he then found his brother, Simon Peter, and brought him to Jesus. We are to witness first to those in our own household.

In bringing Nathanael to Jesus, Philip said, "Come and see." He had been with Jesus. He knew and loved him. He eagerly invited another.

A young boy once asked his father what a certain prized trophy was. The father decided that the best way to tell him about it was to show him one. He took the important award from his trophy case and showed it to the boy. This was better than all the words he could ever use in describing it.

When we want someone to know Christ, we do not

just tell him about him; we introduce him to Christ. We can do this only if we have had a real experience with him, if we know him ourselves.

As we care for our own families, witnessing to them and winning them to Christ, and as we love our Christian kinsmen, we "behold our sons" and "behold our mothers."

22. "After You"

"I thirst" (John 19:28).

Read John 19:26-30; Mark 15:22-34;
Luke 23:32-43.

ONLY after he cared for others did Jesus think of his own personal needs. In his intercessory prayer, recorded in John 17, he prayed for himself first. But even in this he was thinking of others. His life was lived and given for others.

In crucifixion a sedative drink was usually given the one to be executed to make the pain more bearable. But Jesus refused this. His Father had given him work to do, and this was not yet completed. He must remain alert. The cup of suffering must be drunk to the bitter dregs. He had yet to pray for his tormentors, to respond to the dying thief, to comfort his mother and John, to fulfill prophecy regarding circumstances of his death.

In completing his work on the cross many issues were taken care of. He became sin and suffered for us, thus alleviating sin and suffering—physical, emotional, intellectual. Guilt was dealt with, for on the cross he forgave. Romans regarded crucifixion as a most despicable death and used it only for criminals and slaves.

To die in this manner was to die for the worst of criminals and for all who deserved this most cruel and horrifying death. His clothes were taken from him, and in his nakedness he suffered humiliation. Thus, on the cross any humiliation we may ever have was eased and cared for.

The hours of suffering of spirit as he hung on the cross surpassed physical suffering. Plunged to the bottom of a pit of despair, he felt the Father had forsaken him. Only after coming up from such a terrible abyss could he give attention to his bodily suffering. Only when he had provided for the sin and suffering of all the world and when the end was in sight was he conscious of his needs. Then he spoke words of physical torment in his own behalf. In life and in death he loved and was concerned for others, thinking first of them.

Can we always think of others first, even in our suffering? This requires greater love for others than we have for ourselves. Only in this kind of love do we have perfect relationships. And this love comes from God. We need him in every relationship to perfect and complete it. Otherwise any nearly perfect relationship will not last. He must be present to encircle, reinforce, and bless all our human ties so that we love enough to consider others first before thinking of our own desires or needs.

23. He Speaks To You

"Jesus said to her, 'Mary.' She turned and said to him in Hebrew, 'Rabboni!' (which means Teacher)" (John 20:16).

Read John 20:11-18; 10:1-16; 1 Kings 19:1-16.

HERE is real communication. Jesus spoke Mary's name and she knew his voice. Earlier when he spoke to his disciples, he told them that he, being the Good Shepherd, knows his sheep by name and that they know his voice and follow him. God, through Christ, spoke to Mary that day.

We read in the Old Testament of God's speaking to Moses, the prophets, and others. At one point in Elijah's struggle to prevent the establishment of Baal worship and the destruction of Jehovah worship in Israel, it was necessary for him to flee for his life. He was discouraged and disheartened. There was nothing more he could do. He surrendered completely to God.

When God spoke to him, he learned there was something more he could do. He followed God's instruction and Israel was strengthened, Baal worship was destroyed, and Jehovah worship was restored.

Mary Magdalene was also in despair. Her Master was dead, and she didn't know where he was. She didn't know what to do. When the resurrected Jesus spoke, she no longer was desolate and he told her what to do.

Our God is capable of great and mighty things, for he is all-powerful. Before he spoke to Elijah there was a great wind, an earthquake, and a fire; but God's voice was not in them. His voice was a "still small voice," but Elijah heard him. He spoke to Mary through one whom she supposed was the gardener, but when she heard him, she knew him.

Does God speak to people today? If so, how does he speak? Do they hear him? He speaks through his Word. When we read it thoughtfully, reverently, prayerfully—sincerely desiring to know his truths for our lives—we hear God.

There is blessed sweet communion when God speaks in time of prayer when we pray in faith believing and within his will. In times of quiet meditation and in times of great inspiration, God speaks through our intellect, our lofty thoughts, and through our talents.

There is beauty all around us to see and hear. The song of a bird, the face of a child, the smile of a friend—all say, "God is near, and he cares." He speaks in many ways—depending on our ability to hear.

In the midst of life's problems and complexities we must listen carefully to hear the sometimes "small voice" of God. In the clamor and din of our world, listening is not easy. Sometimes we hear the wrong voices. We hear too many voices at once. We go the wrong way. So many things seem right. Jesus said there are few who find the right way.

To avoid frustration, disappointment, and despair let us give our lives to God, listen continually for his voice, and act on the guidance we receive when he speaks. Our lives will have more purpose and be more pleasing to him. Rejoice and thank him, for he will show us and tell us what more we can do.

24. An Emmaus Way

"The doors being shut where the disciples were, . . . Jesus came and stood among them and said to them, 'Peace be with you' " (John 20:19).

Read John 20:19-22; 16:22-24; Luke 24:13-35.

NO ONE had knocked. No one had opened the door, but there he stood in the midst of the disciples. Christ can go through any closed doors—even the doors of our hearts. Jesus can come to us anywhere. Anywhere can be an "Emmaus Way."

"Jesus came suddenly, out of nowhere into the very midst of life at its most real and inescapable moments," said Frederick Buechner in speaking of Jesus' appearance to the two on the road to Emmaus after his resurrection. "Not in a blaze of unearthly light, . . . but at supper time, or walking along a road . . . Emmaus is whatever we do or wherever we go to forget that the world holds nothing sacred. . . . If we live, not from one escape to another, but from the miracle of one instant to the miracle of the next—what we may see is Jesus himself. . . . He is there through all our doubts and being afraid, through all our indifference and boredom, . . . and we know for sure that everything makes sense, for it's in God's hands."*

Christ was present with the disciples to bless. Then he said, "Peace." They were glad that Jesus was with them again. He told them that their joy would be full. It wouldn't pass away and no one could take it from them. He imparted the Holy Spirit to them, and they knew the sweetness of some of his fruits—peace and joy. Then Jesus sent them into the world. Because Jesus was resurrected and had given the disciples power and a commission, their labor would not be lost or in vain.

As Christians we have the gift from God of every good thing for whatever he wants us to do. Our work for Christ is not in vain, for we too have joy and peace. His commission is one of peace, not of strain. We are never asked to do anything we are not able to do, and with the temptation of weakness we are given an escape. We have adequate resources. Peace is very important to Christians, for it is said to be the conscious possession of these resources, and it is the very core of our beings.

If the world is too much with us and we find ourselves often on the way to Emmaus, trying to forget that earthly life has nothing of lasting worth, let us know that Christ has appeared and given us the bread of life. Let us always recognize his presence through the Spirit he has given.

*From *The Magnificent Defeat* by Frederick Buechner. Copyright © 1966 by Seabury Press, Inc. Used by permission.

25. Only Believe

"Then he said to Thomas, 'Put your finger here, and see my hands; and put out your hand, and place it in my side; do not be faithless, but believing.' Thomas answered him, 'My Lord and my God!' " (John 20:27-28).

Read John 20:24-29.

THE determining factor in Christian faith is how one answers questions about Christ. What do you think of him? Whose son is he? Is he all-powerful, everywhere present? Can he heal body and control circumstances? Does he forgive sin? Is he the way to God, the Father?

Christ's deity is the foundation of Christian faith. To doubt to the extent of denying or disbelieving is to invalidate the structure of all Christian teaching, to make vain Christ's saving work in his life, death, and resurrection.

Thomas was a doubter. He was proud and temperamental with, perhaps, an obstinate streak that did not allow him to give in easily. But he was completely devoted to Jesus. Earlier, on the occasion of the raising of Lazarus in Bethany, when Thomas heard that Jesus was going there, he feared the worst. He felt that for

Jesus to go so near Jerusalem meant certain death. He said to the other disciples, "Let us also go, that we may die with him" (John 11:16).

Even though we are loyal followers of Jesus, it is possible that we, too, sometimes doubt. When we read God's Word but don't really hear or believe what he is saying, we are doubters. When we hear wonderful testimony of God working in someone's life and explain it away through mere human understanding, we are doubters. When in illness we pray for healing and when it comes give overmuch credit to medicine taken, we are doubters. In a hard situation we pray for divine guidance. Then when a fresh, new, clear-cut idea comes and we fail to act on it, thinking it to be only finite mind which does not always function too well, we are doubters. To be insensitive to divine intervention and to discount in this manner is to seriously doubt and to deny the power of God through Christ to save.

Jesus' rebuke of Thomas' unbelief and the creating of faith within him was so powerful that Thomas' frightening doubts were lifted to the highest point of belief, praise, and worship. Because of the glory of God through Christ shining suddenly in his soul, he earnestly proclaimed the deity of his Lord and God.

Just as Jesus challenged Thomas to make a life choice between stubborn pride and obedient faith, he wants us to make a similar choice. By God's grace we can, for he has implanted the image of himself within us. He reveals himself according to our need.

As we continue in truth as followers of Jesus we cannot, we must not, be faithless, but believing. Paul Rader, the songwriter, said, "Only believe. All things are possible, only believe."

26. Wait Patiently

For Him

"Simon Peter said to them, 'I am going fishing.' . . . They went out and got into the boat; but that night they caught nothing" (John 21:3).

Read John 21:1-3; Luke 5:1-11; John 15:1-6.

PETER was a fisherman, but he was not always a successful one. This was his lifework, and it was from this that Jesus called him to fish for men, to be instrumental in bringing them into his spiritual kingdom.

But Jesus was gone, and how could Peter and the other disciples follow him? Even though Jesus Christ was resurrected and had appeared to them, breathing power on them (20:22), they were bewildered. A little later when the Holy Spirit would come to guide, they would know better what they were to do (16:13). But they did not fully comprehend the power and working of the promised Holy Spirit. So why wait?

Peter, an impulsive man of action and much energy, could not just wait and do nothing. So he decided to go fishing. This he knew. This he could do. He returned temporarily to his old familiar occupation. And some of the others went with him. "But that night they caught nothing."

Is God's will sometimes unclear for us? Doubtless Christians everywhere have felt this uncertainty at times, no matter how dedicated we may be. We read his word and we pray, but still no definite direction comes. We know that God always answers the prayer of one who comes to him in sincerity of faith believing. But what we ask must be within his will. Someone has said, "God always answers prayer. He says, 'Yes,' 'No,' or 'Wait.' "

So perhaps it is sometimes necessary for us to wait. We may work in some good cause thinking that surely it is in God's will, for it is helping people come into a closer walk with God. But we need help in our planning and efforts. So we pray and we wait. The Apostle Paul tells us not to be weary in well-doing, for we will be rewarded if we don't faint (Gal. 6:9).

So we continue working as we have been doing or at something else also necessary and constructive. As Peter was in his fishing, we are nearby and available to God when he speaks, guiding us into the way he would have us go.

But we dare not become impatient, abandon hope, and act on our own decisions. When we depend solely on our human methods and abilities, we find ourselves toiling without success, without "fish." We must open ourselves to the light and healing power of God, always seeking his will, or we catch nothing. When we look to him for direction, follow in obedience, and expect to receive what he has promised, our waiting soon ends and we have success.

27. Cast Your Net
On The Right Side

" 'Cast the net on the right side of the boat, and you will find some [fish].' So they cast it, and now they were not able to haul it in, for the quantity of fish" (John 21:6).

Read John 21:4-6; Luke 5:4-6;
Matthew 6:25-34.

IN the miraculous feeding of the five thousand, Jesus instructed the people to sit down, and, when he had thanked God for the food, he distributed it among them. They received their meal directly from him. As we relax and meditate, pray and study his word, God gives us spiritual food directly.

One of my concerns in Christian writing is that I will think on the things of God, pray and read the Scriptures enough to be sustained spiritually and, out of the abundance that he gives be able to share. Otherwise, I am "dry" and have not much to give. When we go to God for spiritual needs, he cares for our other needs as well. We are told to seek his kingdom first and our earthly, bodily needs will also be met, for out of his glorious riches in Christ all our needs come (Phil. 4:19).

We must never forget that God is interested in the little things of our lives as well as the big ones and that where he directs us is always the right side.

Several years ago I lost a valuable wrist watch, a cherished gift. Much concerned, I tried to locate it by inquiring at the market where I had shopped. I retraced the route I had taken, thinking perhaps it had fallen from my wrist in signaling for a turn. I pictured it ground to bits by passing cars. I reported the loss to the police. They came to my home for a description. Several months elapsed with no news of my watch and I nearly despaired of seeing it again.

One day while preparing the evening meal, I received a clear message. The house was still and no one else was there. No one had spoken, but these definite words were in my ears: "Go to the potato bin."

Since we do not use many potatoes, I did not often open the bin, but when I looked, there was my beautiful watch! I had bought potatoes that day. The watch had dropped in the bin as I dumped the potatoes in. God had directed me. This was the right side.

We may wonder how God can care about little, seemingly unimportant things when he is responsible for the whole universe. But we know he is concerned with little things, for we have seen the intricate details of his creation. And he can and will supply our needs, for he is a gracious, loving God. We have seen evidence of his love and abundance in the lush things of nature he has created, even in remote wooded areas where scarcely anyone sees. Little things are as important to him as big ones.

Someone has said, "Take care of the little things; then the big things will take care of themselves."

Remember that if a care is big enough to be a burden, it is big enough to pray about, or if it is too small for prayer, it is too small to be a burden. So if we seek and find God's help in the "little things," this paves the way for the "big things," making them go more smoothly. But if a small trouble is not properly dealt with, it may turn into big trouble. Let's make all our requests known to God so that we may receive his blessing.

28. Sit, Not Jump

"When Simon Peter heard that it was the Lord, he . . . sprang into the sea. But the other disciples came in the boat, dragging the net full of fish" (John 21:7-8).

Read Luke 10:38-42; Matthew 6:6-13.

"I INTEND to attend every session!" I declared positively to the other women in a planning meeting.

Later, I thought perhaps I had been selfish, but for a long time I had been hungering to be filled with God's righteousness. In the coming meetings that were planned for our church I felt there would be much in spiritual growth for me—for everyone. As a result of the help I received, my true selfhood in Jesus Christ was awakened, and life became more meaningful and joyous. I was on the way to my identity with Christ, my Savior.

A special teacher, a tremendous man of God, was called for this weekend series. Much work was necessary to help make the meetings possible and beneficial to a large number of people.

The speaker requested a fellowship dinner the first night for rallying the people. Nursery care was provided during this and all sessions so that young parents could be helped by the teaching. Much time was spent in planning, preparing, and serving the meal, table setting and decorations, clearing away and washing dishes. Women of the church were responsible for this and several were involved in providing nursery care.

These activities required the help of nearly all the women and some had no time to attend any of the meetings. This work was important and they seemed satisfied. But I felt they had missed the "good portion."

When Jesus visited in the home of Martha and Mary of Bethany, he told Martha that her sister had chosen the good portion in sitting at his feet to listen to his teaching. She loved him, believed in him, and hungered to hear what he would impart. What she received was something lasting that could not be taken away.

Martha loved him, too, but she was occupied with the important activities and duties of the homemaker and hostess.

At another time when Jesus was in Bethany, Mary was criticized by a disciple for using expensive ointment to anoint the head of Jesus. He thought it should be sold, and the money given to the needy. Jesus told him they would always have the poor, but he wouldn't always be with them. Of Martha's anxiety over many things he could have said, "You'll always have cooking and housework to do."

The world is always with us with its duties and cares. We need to cherish precious times with our Lord in moments of quiet and meditation in individual and group study and prayer. They are so quickly and easily snatched away by rambling thoughts and the urgency of the needs of the hour.

Peter loved his Lord but he was impulsive and some-times impractical. On the occasion of the heavy catch of fish to which Christ had directed them, he forgot everything else and sprang into the sea to get to Christ more quickly. By wading to shore, Peter was no help to the more practical ones who remained with the boat to bring in the bulging net. We read, too, of Peter's other impulsive acts, such as the cutting off of Malchus' ear. A deterrent to such impulsiveness requires self-discipline, self-control.

There are times in our Christian experience when we need to exercise self-control so that in zeal and love for our Lord we do not unwisely commit some detrimental act. Over-activity in our personal daily lives and also in affairs of the church at the cost of not learning at Jesus' feet also requires self-control. Such control is a fruit of the Spirit. This fruit is our spiritual resource, our available means for successful Christian living.

In order to be practical, accepting the responsibility of doing God's work to produce best results, self-discipline is needed. Yet we need to be ever sensitive to times and means of learning God's ways for us as was Mary of Bethany. Let us sit at Jesus' feet and listen, for what we gain will never be taken away.

29. Bring What You Have

" 'Bring some of the fish that you have just caught.'
. . . 'Come and have breakfast' " (John 21:10, 12).

Read John 21:9-14; Acts 3:1-10.

TRY to imagine how they felt. Peter and the others
had been toiling all night and had caught nothing.
Doubtless they were tired, discouraged, and hungry.
Just at daybreak they saw someone on shore and the
smoke of a fire. Words of encouragement came across
the water from one whom they soon learned was Jesus.
Following his instruction, at last they had many fish.
Besides their interest in seeing him again, it was heart-
ening to have someone prepare breakfast after their
long, weary night.

Jesus told them to bring some of the fish they had
caught so that he might add them to what he had
already prepared. When all was ready, he invited them
to eat. Through this fellowship with Jesus, his ministering to them, and the food, they were comforted and
strengthened and ready to work more vigorously and
cheerfully.

Just as Jesus blessed the disciples, Christ can use our
good works to bless us. He knows that we were created

for good works and he wants us to be zealous in them. We have already been blessed as his followers. If we use what he has provided, he will bless it and increase it.

At the gate of the temple called Beautiful, Peter said to the lame man, "I give you what I have." Christ took it and increased it by strengthening the man's feet and ankles so that Peter could say, "In the name of Jesus of Nazareth, walk." The man not only walked, but he leaped and praised God. It was Peter's faith and life of service that God used to bless and heal.

We know that God does everything completely—not by halves. When he comes to us, he brings all that he has and is. When such as we have meets all that God is, this is sufficient and something happens. Our lives are transformed.

When Jesus says, "Bring what you have," let us give him our entire lives. When he says, "Come and eat," let us partake freely of what he prepares so that we may be sustained and strengthened for the wonderful works he would do through us.

30. Feed Them, Guard Them

" 'Feed my lambs.' . . . 'Tend my sheep.' . . . ' Feed my sheep' " (John 21:15-17).

Read John 21:15-17; Acts 20:17-28;
1 Peter 5:2-4.

ON the hills by the Sea of Galilee the disciples fed five thousand with food that Jesus gave them. Now he tells them to feed the flock with the living bread he has given.

The paramount purpose of the church is not evangelism. God predestined his own to be conformed to the image of his Son (Rom. 8:29). We see that the chief aim of those making up the body of believers is to be like Christ and to help others to be obedient and submissive to him.

The true fulfillment of the disciples' faith is their response to Christ's call to feed his lambs, his sheep. As we grow up in Christ, we are exhorted to give careful attention to our own condition and that of others in God's flock—those young in the faith and those still immature saints. The Holy Spirit has entrusted their spiritual nourishment to us.

Our whole being should be occupied with living the Christian life as a witness to give strength to the greatest of all causes. As part of a local body, Christians should not complain about faults and weaknesses in the church and individuals, but work with them harmoniously. They are headed in the right direction; they are in the right cause.

"Brighten the corner where you are." The local church where you are is your corner. Brighten it by giving your talents, time, and means to support other Christians. We never know how far-reaching our influence may be. It has been said that a person does not die to the world until his influence comes to an end. Thus, Peter, Paul, and others recorded in the Bible still live, for their influence continues as people read and learn from them. They are still feeding and tending the flock of God.

We may think what we have to give is small, but God does not if we are willing and eager to share. As we use our abilities for him, he allows them to grow and become more beneficial to others. You are needed. Why not go all out for God? In sincerity and steadfastness, yield yourself to him. Be prayerful, loving, understanding, optimistic, and cooperative as you serve in helping others to be more Christlike.

As we are dedicated and engaged in tending or guarding the flock, we should avoid the appearance of evil. We might be able to do some things without being harmed by them. But others might be led astray. They see the appearance of evil in the example we are to them and stumble. The principles of Jesus Christ must be strong and lived in purity. It is up to Christians to make such presentation.

In the Ark of the Covenant, the children of Israel carried the symbols of the testimony God had given them in their wanderings, conquering of Canaan and other trials and dangers. This they protected with their lives and transported according to God's instruction. In deep water they lifted it high to avoid damage or destruction.

God has entrusted to us the light of the knowledge of his glory (2 Cor. 4:7). Let us carry high and carefully our banner symbolizing these holy things from God. Let us guard them from being overcome. We are told not to be overcome by evil, but to overcome evil with good. We are thankful for our heritage. May we guard it and pass it on to our children and others, the lambs and sheep of his fold. God loves them all. We must love then, too. Christians, come alive and stand firm, witnessing for him, tending and feeding the flock!

31. "What About Me?"

" 'Lord, what about this man?' . . . '. . . what is that to you? Follow me!' " (John 21:21-22).

Read John 21:20-25; Matthew 16:24-27;
25:31-46; 1 Corinthians 4:1-5;
Revelation 3:11-13.

THE ultimate goal of Christians is to gain eternal life with the Father of love.

When my husband came home one day, I was a little emotional over listening to Bill Gaither's "Going Home," being sung by Doug Oldham. I remarked that I was impressed that he could sing in such a manner because heaven was so real to him.

"He should be concerned with taking others with him," my husband said.

Christians are concerned for others in this regard, but of first importance to them is their own hearts' condition. Are they right with God and eternally acceptable to him? Each is responsible for his own standing.

Jesus said, "I am the way, and the truth, and the life; no one comes to the Father, but by me" (14:6). In order to gain our heavenly home, we must be followers of Jesus Christ, God's Son.

As his followers we die to self daily. Thus in a sense we lose our lives. But we gain new life in and through him that never ends. This is by far the best possible arrangement, worked out by a wise and loving God, for it is unprofitable to live selfishly for this world only at the cost of everlasting life with the Father.

When Christ comes in his glory, we will be repaid individually for what we have done, but we will be kept from the final hour of trial when the world is judged. If we hold fast the things of Christ and endure patiently, we will gain a crown of victory that no one can take from us. Because of our upright hearts, we will have important positions in God's temple on high, and we will never leave it.

As we obey God in love and compassion by ministering to the needs of others here and now, we are also responding in love to our Father who has prepared a kingdom for those who love and serve him. But if we fail to show kindness and become calloused, thinking only of our own desires and needs, love for God and a place in the kingdom are lacking in our experience.

We must guard carefully the purposes of our hearts for these will be disclosed at our Lord's appearing. Jesus told of a certain man who went on a journey and entrusted his property to servants. In rewarding his faithful servants, he said, "Well done, . . . enter into the joy of your master" (Matt. 25:21). Even so, God will commend us if our hearts' purpose is to do well and serve him.

God only is our judge. He judges us as servants and stewards of the things he has entrusted to us, even his mysteries which will be brought to light on the great day of his appearing. Our concern is that we be found worthy. As we give ourselves to God in his service, we will not mind too much if others misunderstand and judge us. As we try to do what God requires, we will have no time for self-condemnation. God sees our mistakes and weaknesses and takes care of them in mercy and grace.

As God is our judge, he is also the sole judge of others. Our responsibility is to tell them of the wonderful plan God has for their lives, to sow seeds of the gospel, watering them with love, encouragement, and help of every kind. What they do with what they receive directly from God is between them and their Maker. We are not to think or say, What about this man? but in self-examination ask, What about me? As we come into a full and right relationship with our Father, let us love and understand others, thus helping them choose whether they will be on the left or right hand. God grant that they will follow Christ and go with us to our heavenly home.